THE SPACE BETWEEN THE LAND & SEA

*Musings on Life,
Spirit, and Beyond*

BY PRIYANKA CHATTERJEE

ART BY AVANTIKA SEN

Illustrations by Avantika Sen

First Edition: February 2024

Also by Priyanka Chatterjee

Between You & Me
*Notes to my 15-year-old self about life,
growing up and the power of spirituality*

To Dadu
(my grandfather)
Your memory is my greatest teacher

The highest form of love we receive is the permission to freely express our stream of consciousness, while the highest form of love we can give is to release that to the world despite our fears so it can harmonize with the universe. My offering here is a simple ode to recognize the often-unspoken words. The words on these pages carry no advice, judgment, or expectation. They are as they are.

The space between the land and sea
Equally in touch with the ephemeral
and the ethereal,
the concrete and the sublime,
the bliss of this very moment
and the life looking at the future,
the cacophony and the stillness
It's fun right here in the middle,
knowing but still staring at the fallacy,
But alas, I turn back,
and dive deep into the sea.

TABLE OF CONTENTS

DIVINE GRACE & DISCONTENT

Am I or I am?
Who am I?
Am I this hand?
Am I these feet?
Am I my eyes or my lips?
Or am I in my hand, and in my eyes and feet?
Am I the kindness in me?
Or am I the feeling itself?
I am...maybe that's where I leave it.

Half-Lived Lives
Look around
A beeline of half-lived lives
Some old and grim,
Aware of the impending completion
Some young and restless
Fighting the resistance, the war within
Despite the differences
There lies a distinctive commonality
A beating heart synchronous with the light of the
soul
Repeatedly calling us home.

What Am I Missing?
Why is there no joy
Even though I have the world
The setting sun and the dark clouds,
are staring at me
They remind me that I need to find it,
But where is it lost?
Is it a victim
of my desires and ambitions?
Or of my home and the things I have filled it with?
Is it in everything and everywhere,
But I just don't see it?

Stillness
The speak of consciousness,
Or is it a language of its own?
Every stone, every leaf, every petal,
Every human face,
No matter how disparate in its form and dharma,
Is speaking in stillness.
Can you hear?

What's This Noise?

We move from one destination to a greener one,
To appease the noise inside
The humdrum keeps saying, it will be happier
"when"
And the "when" keeps evolving,
Moving to an endless goalpost.
And you ask, why am I so anxious?

Inside Out

The noise inside battles the noise outside
Winning seems pointless, but the fight is on.
There is no respite
My emotions try and manage the outside,
But the one inside is ruthless and constant,
In the minutiae of the world and in the silence of
my sleep.
I mix up the two often.
Wait, who is seeing these two as different?
Should I focus on the seer instead?

Feeling Small

Every so often
I feel so small
That my heart opens.
I stay there for a fleeting second,
I don't want to let go of feeling small
I catch myself thinking
And boom! I am back to my small little bigness
I wait for grace to visit me again.

Whole Day
The mind is fictional
Thoughts aren't real
Worries are mostly made up
Our crises are man-made
That's all of my day
All non-real.

Bigger & Better
The size of the house grows
The cars increasingly smell of luxury
The clothes have a crispiness to them
But I carry the same me through it all
The despair remains,
The search goes on.
Bigger and better fills the void, temporarily.
Then back to the void.
Even Bigger and Even Better propose a solution.
I fall for it.
Again.

The Familiar

The spirit soars like an eagle
It looks at the mountaintop
And smiles in anticipation
A déjà vu, a familiarity
Yes, I have been here before.

No Control

Get out of the door
When all are in slumber.
Move as the leaves,
In a gentle breeze.
Every move unaware of
Where it'd go next.
But it will, sooner or later.
No one to care for
No one to answer to
Carrying just the inkling
The throbbing direction of life.

The Restless

We are here to be, in its trenches and valleys
Pampered in love, teary in grief
Anxious in ambition, restless in discontent
I will take all of it and more
I will just be.

Switch

I want it
But I don't.
Maybe all I need is a switch
or a pause
whichever is easier.

Orange Sky

Magical hue spreads across the sky
The orange, the red, the empty
Why do you look at me like you know me?
You speak to me in words never spoken before
I respond with words I do not know.
Your beauty resonates with the stillness of my
heart
You seem to be a long-lost friend
Take me with you
Take me through the orange, the red, the empty
and pervade my soul.

Relentless Questions

I am going down this road
Asking the questions of life that I never thought I'd
ask,
The questions are coming to me,
just like the answers appear within,
It's splendidly weird, and extremely bewildering.
My soul stirs with each question,
With each answer, there is a peace
I keep asking, I will keep asking,
till the questions end or I become one with the
answer.
For in the questions lie the discovery of life,
The answers are not as important as much as the
rising of the questions,
And the ensuing pursuit of the answers.

Who Wants Famous?

The mind says
I gotta be famous
I keep peeling the onion
I arrive at nothingness.

It's hard
It's really hard to live the minutiae of life
While being life itself.

Aura
Why do you take on the Sun's halo when it moves
on?
That fleeting period between light and darkness,
Holding our hands through the period of
transition.
Are you really the hues we see?
Or are you just emptiness?
Envious of your stillness and ethereal beauty I ask,
Who are you?
Are you Sun's friend, companion, and confidante?
Or are you yet another ignored reminder to us to
just stop,
just pause the rush.
And take this moment in?

White Knight
Shining boldly in a clear dark sky,
There is no remorse in your eyes,
You exude a divine light
a constant reminder through the darkness,
That living in it is alright.
Giving space to the passing clouds,
You remain a spectator,
Through everything you remain still.
Guiding us through the darkest period,
You are nature's true reminder...
We are here to survive with hope, stillness, and
divinity,
Through the vagaries of life.

Mighty Depression

The tension in the arm,
sensitivity at the base of the spine,
tinkle at the back of the leg,
The twitched brow, the curved smile,
relentless falling back on a feeling,
mostly a feeling of sad and empty.

What are you trying to say?
Are you trying to come in or get out?
Is anyone there....

Living in a haze, rejoicing in the same,
the pervasive void, waiting for the episode to end.
Glimpses of enormous peace,
followed by a tsunami of restlessness and hollow.
Balancing the precarious act,
while waiting for the next glimpse,
the glimpse of eternity,
the glimpse of being one with the glimpse.

New Year

A new day, the old sun
A new perspective, the old choices
A new life, the old relatives
A new beginning, the ignored opportunities
A new resolution, the old habits
A new love, the old ego
A new earth,
Or is it?

Small Talk
Mind: there is a separation,
a slight crack in the door,
there is light coming through,
I see it, I see it!

Soul: Or is it just you coming through?
where there is separation,
there is awareness,
where there is awareness,
there is light.

Mind: Ah, so the light was always there,
it was the crack I was waiting for!

Soul: Sigh...

One After Another
We move from one destination to a greener one,
To appease the noise inside
The humdrum keeps saying, it will be happier
when...
And the "when" keeps evolving,
Moving to an endless goalpost.
And you ask, why am I so anxious?!

Thump

The burning desire
The constant knock on the door,
Thump, thump, thump
Are you listening to me?
What do I need to do for you to listen?
Give up the mediocrity, it's not worth your soul,
Reach out to me, Reach for me
I am here, I always have,
Have you forgotten, you made a promise,
You must remember to always remember.
Do you really want to leave the earth with a ringing
in your heart?
Do you really want to go with a thump, thump,
thump?

That Which is Not

I miss my clarity during the day,
When the sky is clear, and everything is just bright.
It's the darkness, during the dawn and the dusk,
When the light peeps through the middle of the
clouds,
That's where I centre, that's when I am home.

There is something about darkness, a particular
innocence.
Insecure of its presence, it looks for validation.
Knowing very well that a tiny gleam can make it
look small,
It maximizes its lifetime.

But it takes an intentional soul to recognize the
beauty of darkness,
And its purpose in the tapestry of life.
We would be purposeless without knowing what
the absence of light is,
The absence of happiness is, the absence of a jolly
time is.

It is in the absence of that which is not,
that we realize that which is.

I See Everything

O Universe, I bare my soul to you
But you are my soul
In you, I surrender
Because there is nowhere else to go
You are the serene clouds I so love
You are the leaves that flutter
You are the eyes of the butterfly
And the air I breathe,
You were a stranger to me
But not anymore
You are what I was seeking
Guess I didn't look at the flower longer
Or paused to feel the wind in my face
But I see everything now
Because everything is you.

The Flow
I am a part of it,
but still fighting, struggling to go against.
I am exasperated, I fight some more,
trying hard not to give up.
In a moment of complete despair,
I surrendered completely.
It took me along and there was no looking back,
I kept floating through the rocks and shards,
and the sunsets and the sunrises.

I just kept floating, not fighting, just floating.
Miraculously I reached where I was supposed to.

The Game

Our journey to wholeness is bittersweet in the
knowingness that we are already whole,
We seek when the seeker and the realization of God
are both within,
We have questions when the answers all lie in that
space behind our eyes.
What are we heading to?
Knowing what we already know, seeking what we
already have?
Maybe it is walking the talk of the divinity that we
can be,
Maybe it is doing nothing at all.
In being, we rest,
and cease all questions.

Take Over
My mind is heavy
I feel tired in my bones.
Or am I just resisting this moment
trying to change it to something else
or be somewhere else.

I close my eyes for a little while
not knowing what the next moment will bring.
I take another deep breath
and then another.

I pass control over to my breath
unable to let my mind have the reins anymore.
The moment calms down
in tandem with my breath.

My mind is not heavy anymore
My eyes are...

I allow slumber to take over.

Take over. Take over. Surrender.

Freedom

Ever feel that tinge of jealousy when you see a
homeless person on a bench?
When any bench is for taking and time is of no
essence,
You stay where you stay and then move on.

Or when a bird sips from a puddle of rainwater,
and then perches atop the beautiful oak tree.
When any tree is fair game, and the sky's the limit.

What is that yearning?

We don't settle when we are bound,
but we settle for bondage in the pursuit of freedom.
We are limitless beings living in imagined
boundaries.
We don't want them, but here we are,
creating them, fixing them, decorating them, every
day.

In and Out

I sink down again
myriad of images
from events past and future fears
shackled and chained
freedom is what I seek
And then I feel the tip of my toes
A sudden awareness glistens through my spine
The images are gone, I am free again.

Letting Go
I trust my breath,
I trust my heart,
I trust my conscience
None of those are truly voluntary,
Then why do I have a veil of control over them?

Breaking the Shell
What is this shell I have created?
It's unknowable to me
I want to be this, I want to be that
None my known
Everything for someone else
How long now
When does the shell break
Or do I have to break it
But I am inside, how do I?
Or am I outside,
Watching the whole drama transpire?

Layers

--------------------This is what we pretend what our lives are like

------------ This is where we live our lives

----- We touch this sometimes when we see the sunset or the ocean

---In moments of great alignment, we momentarily touch this part of ourselves

-This is who we are

.Or this

POSTPARTUM MONOLOGUE

Everything I am about to muse on right now, it's
taboo at its best.
Mothers don't feel this way,
We have shoved it under the carpet long enough.
We can talk about this, as bad as the optics seem,
We have played the warrior mothers for
generations, how about something else?
If not for us, for the clueless new mothers puzzled
by the whirlwind.
And at the end of the day when our shirt is wet
from a heavenly mixture of water, poop, and milk,
The best thing in the world is to know,
We are not alone.

The silence is palpable
And so is the deep sense of relief
Nighttime is a saviour
And although I miss some of the cacophony
Oh, does it feel so good to be horizontal for a
change.

This eternal moment
When you are in my arms for the very first time,
Seems so conflicted.
I am sorry baby, but I don't feel much at this
moment
I am crying because I feel like I just climbed a
grand mountain
I am panting but no one cares.
But I see you and I am amazed
But all I feel is tired.

Pain, I feel pain
Everything hurts
But I don't think about me, I can't.
Actually no one can
And no one is.

Dark, just dark
If dark was a feeling,
I am feeling it right now
My body seems mutilated
Not just for the mirror
But even for my own eyes and soul.

I feel lonely
And a little mad
A toxic combination
But I remind myself that it is a phase
It is a phase.

I am just glad,
That I can finally blame
Someone other than me
for my procrastination.

Just pat me on the back,
Yes, I am shallow and vain.
If that is what I need to be
Just pat me still
It's important to me right now.

I scream loudly
Seems to be happening often nowadays
I have resolved to not hide it anymore
The scream is my window,
An open window
And I am going to leap
Whenever the time is right.

I resolve to not recreate my own childhood
But alas I hang my hat there ever so often
It's my solace. Or my redemption?

Birthing is a butterfly moment
You lose who you were
For the promise of new wings and a beauty
unknown
Does a butterfly know it's a butterfly now?

The whole thing may actually be the other way
around
parenting is a phenomenon happening to us,
A huge teaching moment
On responsibility, patience and not swearing in
public.

Love,
I feel none of it right now.
Nada.
I know I love you
But I feel nothing.

I think a lot of parenting
Is just about gaining confidence
Our threshold on whether we are okay, not
knowing, and still moving ahead,
decides if we stay in joy or in misery.

If you haven't done any service
for anyone ever in your life
Become a parent.

Something feels very terminal about this
I don't know what.

I don't want to feed someone,
every day for years to come.
How did I not contemplate this ever before?

6 weeks postpartum
And the happiest I have ever been since delivering
Is joining other moms in despair.
Trying everything and some for their breasts to do
what they are touted to do naturally
Misery loves company has never manifested so
clearly.

Why am I so sad all the time?
Can someone please help?
The mumbo jumbo on the internet is scaring me
And I don't even want to peek into the world of the
juggernaut called postpartum depression.
I have heard bad things about it
And I can do without another bad thing.

Duty or sacrifice
(Mind slap on the wrist)

I look out the window
The sky is bright
The air is pure
The mist on the leaves glistening
But here I am in a closed room
Tied to a tiny human
And I don't like it
And I am scared to talk about it.

Yes, I mentally prepared for it
Yes, I prepared for it financially
And I am still overwhelmed
Yes, yes, yes.

"You are not feeding him right" -
This after nine months of nurturing
Of all the judgments I have been unfazed by
This one hurts
Hurts so bad.

I can't decide on my mask
For the world outside
Brave and unfazed
Or vulnerable and oh so tired
Fuck it, I am going with
"oh so so tired"
So tired to even put on a mask.

I want to really enjoy you
But the paraphernalia sucks
Everything out of me
Everything.

You know what would be great
If my boob could be detached
That should've solved all my life's problems right
now.

I could cry all-day
But that would not change much
Other than cause panic
because then I wouldn't pump three times.

Of all the so-called programming available
How did I not know?
This is going to feel so complex.

To know a love so deep
is a matter of privilege
But the beauty of this realization is that it doesn't
come easy
Long exhausting hours
culminate into a deeply profound moment
That seemingly can rip my heart open.

The embrace of a sick child
on a mother's bosom
brings upon nostalgia
of million past lives
a feeling so primitive and yet so timeless in its
essence.

Language holds no place in
the first two years
I often wondered why
Now I know
Nature wants us to dig deep
and converse beyond the six senses.

How could I have created this human?
It doesn't seem plausible
How seamlessly perfect is the earthly technology
no wires, no circuits
just the divine, human, and something in between.

Sometimes I rock you to sleep
and all I can think of is that glass of red wine.

I agonize because I see you standing
between me and pure freedom
Wonder how things will shift if I don't?

Contrary to what Hallmark says,
The feeling of completeness eludes me.
If anything, I feel torn on the fringes,
with some deep cuts hither and thither.

Love
Big word. Small word.
Right now, it's the most complicated word.

Present is where I want to live
But flashes from the past flow by.
Where I could lie on my couch
and do absolutely nothing.

Nighttime is a saviour
And although I miss some of the cacophony
Oh, does it feel so good to be horizontal for a
change.

Was I meant to be a mother?
Am I a good mother?
What is a good mother?
It's an odd one.
I didn't give birth to any other earthly relation.
What a perplexing thing, this.

I go through the paraphernalia of the day,
Interactions, meetings, small talk,
All the things we do in the world,
to survive, to earn a good living.
And then there is you,
your tiny hands and feet
 destroys the heaviness of the day in mere seconds.
Your smile carries the depth of the ocean
diluting every thought from the day past.
The contrast is baffling,
It's the trance of heavy and light,
the land and sea.
I am whole.

BODY IMAGE

The Release
Our bodies hold a lot
And I am not talking about the food
Where does the judgement go?
Right to the pit of the stomach,
Where does shame and guilt find safe harbor?
The shoulders and the back of course.
And that work thing,
You can find that on the sides of my neck.
We are talking, walking demo of everything we
have decided not to release
The burden is too heavy
Release. Release. Release.

Enoughness
I will be enough when I look like that
When I am that
When I am with someone
When I am better, nicer, stronger
Our enoughness is a magnificent goal
One that's never meant to be.

We are the acorn set to become the oak tree,
the drop that's already the ocean

Our enoughness only belongs to our body and
thoughts
It doesn't belong anywhere for the truth of us
The one that already knows.

We were enough when we were born
We were enough when we felt joy or even broken
We are enough at our very last breath.

Onwards
The relentless thought of the perfect body never
ceases
It just hops from one moment to the other
creating one shame after another
feeding my mind endlessly.

Snippets
I am done living a life for snippets of perfection
I am done wanting their perfection to be my own
I don't need to be anything.
But who do I tell that to?
Wait, do I need to tell anyone?

10/10
If I was a 10,
Would I stop worrying?
Wait, is there ever a 10?
Is 10 a carrot manufactured by our mind,
How would I know?
By reaching the 10 of course,
But wait, again, is there ever a 10?

Wholeness
Why do I not feel whole?
There are bruises and marks all over
They are not mine
But they belong to us nevertheless.
Every death, every rape, every judgment in the world,
Makes me less and less.

Look Deeper?
What if our pursuit of the perfect bodies
is a symptom of our unknown creations
An unborn masterpiece that's screaming to be made,
A life-changing story waiting to be told,
Perhaps a call to be a mother
Or a far cry not to be one
What if our body image is just a red flag,
to look deeper,
and find the real hurt.

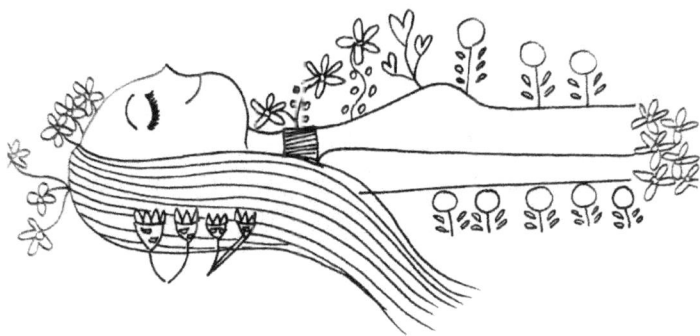

The Road to Dad

I see the road to your lap so clearly,
The long-winded red brick road, with tulips, roses,
your favorite flowers,
It calls out for me whenever I pass by,
Then why do I hesitate to take this road?

The other roads are similar,
They don't offer me the love that the red brick road
does,
but it offers other stuff that seem worldly,
I don't hesitate to plunge on those roads.

I can see you sitting at the end of the road,
Waiting on your rocking chair,
You have been waiting for me,
Our eyes meet and I can see the longing in your
eyes,
as you can see the longing in mine.

I have had these moments before,
But I still take the other roads,
Deep within I know I will always find you there,
At the end of the road on your rocking chair,
waiting for me.

I did the same today,
But in a fleeting moment of despair, I ran back to
the brick road,
But I can't see you sitting on your rocking chair,
I run, I run on this road that always invited me but
I never gave in,
But you are not here anymore,
He is not here anymore.

I sit on the rocking chair and stare down the red
brick road...the road to Dad.

You and I

I have known you all my life,
No, I think I have known you all the way,
As years pass by and the shades of grey grace our
costumes,
We realize the single constant in our journey
together
The I in me and the I in you,
They merge sometimes, like I wouldn't know one
from the other,
We get a glimpse of the bigger truth in our daily
lives
It's really the same I
the I in me and the I in you.

Ollie

It's not your face I talk to,
But the formless cloud of your essence that I feel
entwined in mine,
Where your furry four-legged body becomes
immaterial,
Except for the twinkle of your eye.

Love Lost

When the grief of losing someone, inexplicably completes you.

When pain of love lost, is the most in love you have ever felt.

When gutted is the most alive you have been in a long time.

When a few memories outlive your entire reality.

Middle Ground

I can compromise
But then who do I become
Would you like this version of me?
In the long run, is it not better that you live your truth and I live mine.
Yes, there will be struggles,
But our truths will be satiated
What can be a higher freedom than that?

Aging

I watch my kin age,
At a certain point, I wait for the end
Not because I want the end
But I am tired of worrying and agonizing
I take comfort in the only certainty humankind has
And alas, I make this about me too.

Success Disguised

Watching the hues of the sunset,
Walking barefoot on lush green grass,
Smelling the earth on a rainy day,
Receiving the support of an old friend,
Feeling the comfort of a hot cup of tea,
Reading a great book &; taking something away
from it,
Sharing someone's grief,
Helping your parents see the world,
Tending to the beautiful garden,
Filling up water in the birdfeeder,
Listening to silence,
Saying a kind word,
Traveling to the unknown,
Accepting uncertainty,
Having a fresh perspective,
Giving in all its forms,
What is success if not...

Retirement
I wonder
What do our jobs become when we retire?
Another attachment to hold on to?
The quintessential legacy for the generations to come?
The memories to sustain us for the rest of the time?
Or the key subject to unlearn and 'unlive' so we return to the self at the end?
All the above? Maybe none...

Worry
When life seems chaotic
I slowly drink some water
I focus on the fluid traveling through my veins
Life seems less chaotic now.

Simple Things

I traveled all around, through the uphill mountains,
the clouds,
the magnificent palaces, the expensive theme parks,
man-made structures, that ironically, give you a
better view of the world...
By the grace of life, I have seen a lot.

But why does my soul still yearn?
It yearns for my mother's hand on my hair,
listening to my father's anecdotes,
breathing the air when the family is together on the
porch,
the cup of tea that holds the wisdom of life,
the fluttering of leaves that resonates with my
beating heart,

It yearns for the grounded feeling of the rocking chair
facing the sun
the calming strength of my grandfather's words,
the sound of tea being sieved into my favorite cup,
the warmth of my partner's arms,
the weathering pages of my choiced books,
the conversations that invoke a more authentic self,
It yearns for the rush in the smallest acts of kindness,
and the small moments when we live for something
bigger than ourselves...

Vis-a-Vis
Where sunsets don't mean much,
Where water is dispensable,
Where air is used as an invisible dump yard,
What's the worth of gratitude?
Once we have taken the five elements for granted,
What's the mother's love or the beauty of
hydrangeas?
What's a mundane day without a mishap or the
exquisite taste of honey?
What's a baby's coo or the divine process that
made her?
Something's gotta give in this chase.
Maybe we have.
Every day we ignore an apparently dull moment
bearing the answers to our deepest burns.
"I am busy, I gotta go."
And the burn continues...

Books

Books are mythical creatures,
They tend to find us,
Drawing our fingers to the right shelves, the right little nooks,
And tell us stories we need to hear at that very moment in the cosmos.
They become a part of the karmic tapestry, a part of the divine puzzle of why we choose our joys and sufferings in these specific costumes.
They get absorbed in us, modifying our vibration,
Now the next book is just ready to find us.

A Rendezvous

We sit on jute chairs, facing each other,
the cup of tea steaming the ambiance.
There is grass beneath our feet,
the clear sky with the magnificent stars above us.
The birds sipping on the clay pot nearby,
The violet petunia stands in stillness.
We don't say a word,
we just take in the silence.
But we clearly recognize the moment,
the moment where everything we needed was right
there.
There was nothing urgent, nothing less important,
And there was love.

Those Emails

As friends, family, and colleagues pass away,
I am reminded how 'nothing' everything really is.
The fullness of our lives is laden with nothingness
at its core
The few moments of kindness are all it comes
down to.
People remember laughs, snorts, and anecdotes.
What about those emails and excel sheets?
Which bucket of memories do they make?

Balance

Creation built death to balance out mind's
flippantness.
For every question, confusion, sense of
achievement,
self-doubt, fear, and despair,
Death just stands stoically and watches intently,
"They may say they are so very real, but I am the
only certain."

Love
I find myself in the silence of your breath,
in the rising and falling of it,
I find myself in the words you never speak,
I find myself when my fingers run through your
hair.
When time has no meaning left,
neither does my name as an identity nor my
physical body,
I find myself in the sparkle of your eyes,
in that deep awareness within us that knows,
I find myself in the spaciousness I constantly feel
in my heart,
I find myself in love...

Dance
Every relationship, even the most intimate
Dances between expectations formed and met.

Modern Marriage
Different rooms,
Different masks
Our hearts adjoint,
We take steps backward
One step away at a time.
The cracks are palpable
The heart remains unbroken
A sombre solace, yet so heartbreaking.

TRAVEL FOLKLORE

Dear **Andes**, did I do okay?
You are asking me questions and listening for
answers,
I'd say you did okay.
What is life all about?
Magnificence. Reach for magnificence in love.
Look around me. We are all love, it's all love.

Sitting under the **Christ the Redeemer**
My entire life flashes by
The good, the bad and the ugly
Engulfed in these arms, I don't have to pretend
It's all good as it has come to this moment
Blessed, thankful for this life
For love, for life.

I feel so small, yet so big
I feel like air, and then so alive O **Patagonia**
The paths that brought me here cannot be mine.

I am feeling paradise
My heart is perpetually expansive
It's like love is a liquid that is gushing out of my
heart as
well as my diaphragm
Tears well out, I don't know why,
I am so overwhelmed,
by the white sand, the blue ocean, and the seagulls,
The **Gulf of Mexico** has shown me paradise
today.

River Nile, the mother,
The arteries and the veins
You grow where nothing can grow,
You saturate the arid
Your love flows into nooks and crannies
Gifting live to millions
What is God, if not?

Climbing through magical steps
The vista takes your breath away
Who made you **Machu Pichu**?
What made you?
The clouds protect your secret
While the lamas laugh at our conspiracy theories
They wonder, what if these fools could just trust
Just take it all in
They would see, we were made by the same
That we are the same.

I wanted to experience majestic
Then I met **Iguazu**
I could try to fathom the wonder
But I can't
It's too much to gather
The mind isn't forming the right words
So, I shut down and just see.
And that's all.

Love is in the air
It's the **Taj Mahal**
But there is also despair
Sacrifice and immense grief
Of love lost and the celebration of memories that
haunt
Love is so many things
The dimensions present during the vagaries of life
Until it encompasses it all.

CONVERSATIONS WITH GOD

Up in the air
Up in the air is where I
Say my prayers,
Amongst the soul blue and the ethereal clouds
is where I feel closest to myself,
Secretly believing that my words are closer to their
destination,
I subtly ask,
Where would you have me go?
What would you have me do?
I stare at the clouds passing me by,
And I know, I know they have heard me
Reflecting the expanse of my heart,
I hear them whisper, loud and clear,
"Be right where you are...."

Magic
The tingling energy
That which you cannot touch
It resonates with every cell in body
And purifies it one by one
Whose love it O 'Mother
Is it yours, is it mine, is it everyone's?

I Am Here, Are You Here?
Look within you
I reside in you
You honor me, every time you acknowledge me
Not through the temple or the church
But just by your awareness of your breath
Messages that you so long
Will all come in due time
You are the on the path that I have asked you to be
on
Just express whenever you are driven
Find your own expression and enjoy this life
You will lose nothing
Just be grateful, be amused.

Godtalk
Look at me. The universe still has your back.
Drop the oars. Float for some time.
You will shift.

Universal Love
I bare my soul to you
But you are my soul
In you, I surrender
Because there is nowhere else to go
You are the serene clouds I so love
You are the leaves that flutter
You are the eyes of the butterfly
And the air I breathe
Oh universe, you were a stranger to me
But not anymore
You are what I have been seeking
Guess I didn't look at the flower long enough
Or paused to feel the wind on my face
But I see everything now
I see you in everything
And every stone reflects your essence.

Is This the Right Job For Me?
This job is the medium I have gifted you,
To experience humility, compassion,
To witness the pursuit of convergence of another
spirit with their human form.
And to be neutral.
Anytime you feel defensive, or anxious
Just breathe and know this is a gift.
Be neutral.
Is This My Path?
But you are here right now
That's all that matters.

Why Am I Here?
You are here to live this experience called life
But your specific contract was to heal and teach.

I Just Want My Life To Be Worthwhile
You just have to LIVE it in order for it be
worthwhile
You cannot fail that endeavor
The only way you will fail is if you don't live fully
Live each day as a gift, that's it.
Love and you will be released.
Everything is just love,
If it's not, it's your ego.

THE QUINTESSENTIAL PURPOSE

The Burden

What if I spend my entire life in the pursuit of
purpose?
Finding, seeking, pining, wallowing,
But not living.

The Pebble

What is the purpose of a pebble?
I pick it up, look at it from all sides, and wonder,
What's so special, it's just a mere pebble.
But is purpose, an equivalence of special?
Or is it a fiction of the mind, our ego playing
games?
Could mere presence be special enough? Is 'mere'
truly mere?
Is there a magnificence in mere that eludes us?
What if the fact that we are merely here is
magnificent enough?

Backwards

The more we enforce meaning and purpose into
our jolly little lives
Perhaps we push away both a little further each
time,
Do we need their burden in our already full lives?
Perhaps, we fulfill our meaning in those moments
When we don't think of them at all.
How funny would that be?

The Dance

The desire to be my full potential,
Clashes sheepishly with my desire to be important.
The slow dance turns into a cha-cha-cha soon,
And I give in to what's easiest,
And it's always, always...a slow surrender to the
ego.

The Path

Every so often, the knock comes unexpectedly,
"Are you on your path?"
I wonder who really wants to know that
Something tells me, it's not really me.
Then, who?

Was It Worth It?

The searching, seeking, wandering,
What if it's all a farce?
What if it was all a tease?
Maybe there never was a destination,
But just the beauty of the search.
The agony of not knowing,
and joys and sorrows on the way,
It was all worth it,
It would all be worth it,
Won't it?
Please say it will.

Remembering

I remember asking the waves
to return love of unknown power
How would a 13-year-old know,
The power of ruffling leaves
The immense power of the essence of a leaf
& to recognize herself to be the same as the leaf
and the root
That's the marvel of human life remembering why
it took form.

My Life Or Is It?
What is this shell I have created
It's opaque to me
I want to be this, I want to be that
None my known
Everything for someone else
How long now?
When does the shell break?
Or do I have to break it?
But I am inside, how do I
Or am I outside,
Watching the whole drama transpire?

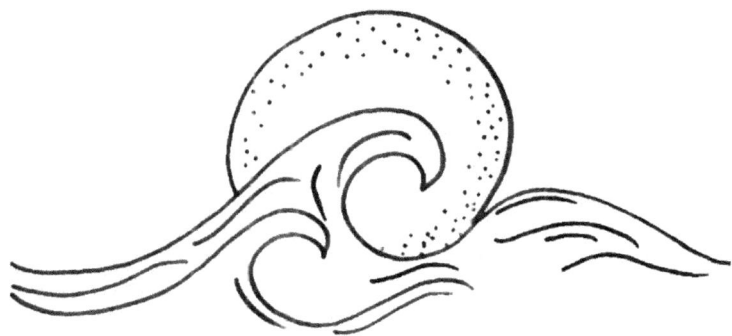

Living Up
Everything in this moment
challenges me hard
"Could you just be here now?"
"Could you?"
My heart grows heavier as I ratchet up intense
clarity
that the answer doesn't live up to the moment's
expectations.

Do You Hear?
There is no respite
in any journey or destination
Just the feeling of loss
Loss of knowing that I am
unable to heed my soul's implore
There is no permission
in the face of numerous chores that I bring as a
decoy
There is just the constant knock,
and my denial of it
My greatest punishment is,
being both the observer and the participant in this
game...

Glimpses of Eternity

I am busy, oh so busy,
In this little titbit-ness of my life,
when going to work, paperwork, paying the bill
The laundry and the dishes seem to fill me up to
the brink.
And then there are those moments,
That millisecond worth of a moment,
When the heart seems to open, open so large that
it's hard to breathe,
That moment of pure clarity,
that all my busyness is pure farce
that everything I know or hope to know in the
future is an unimaginative waste of my time
that who is standing and who is watching knows
everything there is to know
And I am whole.
And then I am not anymore.
I wait for the next bout...

Brahman

I watch my breath, starting and ending, in a
continuous loop.
This giving and receiving with the universe
continues.
So, while I keep questioning my existence,
this conversation remains untouched by any
cynicism.
I ask "Who am I"
The universe says, "You are breathing me in, what
else can you be?"
I ask "What is my purpose", The universe takes a
pause...
"You are no different from me"
"You are the brahman, the entire creation flowing
through your veins. Don't short yourself with
purpose, you are the purpose, you have always
been."

Full Circle

My purpose in life is to explore life's big questions.
To rise above the preoccupation,
to realize life is bigger.
And to experience it. Experience it deeply. And
express my experience of it.
And in the process of the expression,
Perhaps, I will discover myself.

ABOUT THE AUTHOR

Priyanka Chatterjee is a daughter, wife, and mother to Nirvaan. She is also a corporate executive and has worn many leadership hats across Fortune 100 companies. Her writing has focused on reflections on the various phases of life's journey, drawing strength from spirituality and the deeper meaning of life. She gathers inspiration from her immigrant roots in India, finding a home in America, and her travels. She lives in Orlando with her family, including her beloved Bichon, Ollie. Priyanka is the author of *Between You & Me*.

Avantika Sen is a self-trained artist, mother to Iva, and dog mommy to Olaf and Bourbon. Painting mostly in acrylic, her art draws inspiration from nature, deep conversations, and human emotions. She lives in Orlando with her family.

www.ingramcontent.com/pod-product-compliance
Lightning Source LLC
Chambersburg PA
CBHW020509030426
42337CB00011B/307